The CANADIAN BRASS
BOOK OF FAVORITE QUINTETS

Quintet Arrangements at the Intermediate Level
with discussion and techniques

Arranged and Edited by Walter H. Barnes

We are very pleased to present a collection of some of our most requested quintets, including a wide variety of distinct musical styles, from Baroque to Dixieland. For this collection each piece has been skillfully arranged so that it retains the Canadian Brass flavor, but has been made accessible to players at many levels of experience and ability. In addition to the music, we have included a brief historical note about each selection, as well as discussion of specific technical points that will improve your ensemble playing. We sincerely hope that you will enjoy playing these wonderful pieces as much as we have over the years.

The Canadian Brass

Each part is published separately:

Trumpet I in B flat 50488966
Trumpet II in B flat 50488967
Horn in F 50488968
Trombone 50488969
Tuba 50488970
Conductor's Score 50488971
Cassette 50488972

The Canadian Brass has recorded the arrangements in this collection.

Copyright © 1988 Canadian Brass Publications, Inc., Toronto
International Copyright Secured.   All Rights Reserved.

contents

Within an intermediate level these gradations of difficulty are indicated: E=easy, M=medium, D=difficult

a note to you

The opportunity to perform in a brass ensemble is perhaps one of the most significant in a musician's development. In a small group each individual is completely responsible for her or his own contribution to the piece of music being played. Thoughts and concepts come alive in a wonderful way when a musician realizes that four other musicians are depending on a perfect fit of the fifth part. How many times have we all heard that a great basketball or football team depends on "teamwork," but to actually experience that for ourselves through music is thrilling. To be sure we are ready for the experience, we all need to be thoroughly prepared. To help when we work with students, we always spend our time on these important points:

BREATHING: the importance of always taking full breaths
MOUTHPIECE BUZZING: every day, practice and play on the mouthpiece away
    from the instrument
TONE: your "musical fingerprint" is your tone
INTONATION: with two or more performers, intonation is critical
RHYTHM: music based on a strong rhythmic sense will always be more successful
BALANCE: a constant concern of the ensemble musician is being a team player,
    never too loud or too weak
BLEND: the beauty of brass instruments is their great blending ability

ENSEMBLE PLAYING

The real joy of ensemble performance is found when two or more performers can stylistically and sensitively play together; practicing is the quickest way to make this happen. Allow yourself to be free when you perform. Very often your fellow performers will find it much easier to play with you when you move with the music rather than "freezing" your body in place. Also, promote frequent eye contact between all the players in your group.

DOUBLING at the UNISON or OCTAVE

In our book, the French horn and trombone frequently combine at the unison, creating an entirely new sound. This must be diligently practiced by the two instrumentalists so that the style and interpretation (including tonguing, tempo, and intonation) become consistent. The trombone and tuba often double in octaves. When these octaves are perfectly in tune and balanced, a powerful effect results (which is not only very satisfying for the performers, but also for the arranger of this music).

SOLO and SUPPORTING

There are two roles in a brass quintet: solo and supporting. Although your part is always important to the whole, it is not always the solo. We want you to think of the manner in which you perform your part; dynamics, tone colour, length of notes, weight, accents, and projection all play a role in how your part will be perceived by your audience and by fellow players.

BREATHING

All too often, we hear players who try to buzz on the mouthpiece without filling their lungs with air! Sound actually starts with your first deep breath. Air is the basic fuel for the brass performer, and the proper use of this fuel ensures the quality of sound. In our books BEGINNING QUINTETS and EASY QUINTETS, we thoroughly discuss the subject of breathing, and provide exercises for mouthpiece buzzing and use of air. We consider those discussions to be required reading! In our book ADVANCED QUINTETS, we talk further about tone, suggesting that it becomes your "musical fingerprint."

PROGRAMMING

We all spend hours and hours practicing so that we can perform music we love for other people. To help you discover great music and to help you build your own concerts, music with which the Canadian Brass has had great success in public performances has been included in this book. When you put together your own program, you will find here a great range of musical styles. It is possible to experiment with playing the "classical" music of Bach and Handel, right next to early American jazz! And many other selections suitable for inclusion are found in the BEGINNING QUINTETS, EASY QUINTETS and ADVANCED QUINTETS books, all part of our CANADIAN BRASS EDUCATIONAL SERIES. Once you start feeling comfortable with this music, we encourage you to take every opportunity to perform: perform for your friends, for your families, for religious ceremonies, for your school. Just about any place you can think of to play is a good place. And most importantly, have fun with your music.

We have recorded all the selections in this book for your critical listening and study. Very often it is good practice to copy, insofar as possible, what you hear. Once you can fairly well duplicate what you are hearing, you can begin to create your own, new approach to the music. Good luck.

Your friends,

The Canadian Brass

Trumpet Voluntary

JEREMIAH CLARKE
(1673-1707)

Jeremiah Clarke was an English composer and organist at the famous St. Paul's Cathedral in London. He composed two operas, several hymns, and anthems, but the work for which he is best known today is the TRUMPET VOLUNTARY. It was erroneously ascribed to his friend Henry Purcell until 1953, when an English musicologist discovered the true composer. Originally written for organ, the grandeur of this music suited the entrance of the choir into the magnificent chancel of St. Paul's, and was used exclusively for special royal occasions.

It is very important that the first and second Trumpets perform stylistically the same. Rehearse together apart from your quintet to develop the same speed of ornaments (always starting on the note above and ending at the dot). Try to completely match sounds, sharing the brilliant tone that is needed for this selection. We constantly work to play identically in much of our own repertoire. For example, listen to the great TOCCATA and FUGUE in D minor on our Baroque recording; hear the two Trumpets sounding as one.

The Canadian Brass

1. TRUMPET VOLUNTARY

Jeremiah Clarke
(1673-1707)
arranged by Walter Barnes

Bb CORNET/TRUMPET

Copyright © 1988 Canadian Brass Publications, Inc., Toronto
International Copyright Secured.   All Rights Reserved.

Trumpet Tune and Ayre

HENRY PURCELL
(1659-1695)

Henry Purcell was England's greatest composer of the 17th-18th century. He received his early musical education in the choir school of the Chapel-Royal, and at the age of 20 was appointed Organist of Westminster Abbey, the site of England's royal coronations. On his burial tablet in the Abbey it is written:

"Here lyes Henry Purcell Esqr. Who left this Life, and is gone to that Blessed Place where only his Harmony can be exceeded"

Purcell worked for a secularlized Church which had very recently survived the Puritan Revolution. During the Restoration period, in which Purcell wrote most of his music, secular styles of composition were imported from France and Italy by King Charles II. As a court and church composer, Purcell was obliged to write in these new, imported styles. However, some of his earlier pieces reflect the style of his predecessor at the Abbey, Orlando Gibbons. The TRUMPET TUNE and AYRE was originally written for keyboard, and is thought to have come from a harpsichord sonata.

Endurance is a big challenge when playing the TRUMPET TUNE and AYRE. Although we have kept the 1st Trumpet part intact, you may wish to play the 2nd Trumpet part for the 'Ayre,' giving your partner the first part. We often alternate Trumpet parts in the Canadian Brass, finding that it keeps both of us fresher.

Try and breathe without chopping up the melody; four bar phrases are better than two. Perform the 'Tune' crisply, keeping the dotted rhythm very strict (in at least a 3:1 ratio). Contrastingly, the 'Ayre' needs a singing, flowing approach that is seamless between phrases. Be sure to move the tempo right back up to the opening tempo upon returning the 'Tune.' Good luck!

The Canadian Brass

2. TRUMPET TUNE and AYRE

Henry Purcell
(1659-1695)
arranged by Walter Barnes

1st B♭ CORNET/TRUMPET

Copyright © 1988 Canadian Brass Publications, Inc., Toronto
International Copyright Secured. All Rights Reserved.

Canon

JOHANN PACHELBEL
(1653-1706)

Johann Pachelbel was one of the "spiritual ancestors" of Johann Sebastian Bach. Pachelbel was especially renowned for his fugues, variations (chaconnes and passacaglias), and canons. The canon is the most strict form of imitative composition. This CANON is a series of melodic variations (specifically a passacaglia) over a repeated bass line (ground bass). Pachelbel originally wrote 186 melodies above this ground bass, each two bars in length. This particular transcription uses only 20 of those melodies.

"The CANON is perhaps the most famous classical composition ever written, as evidenced by record sales. Unfortunately, Mr. Pachelbel is no longer around to collect the incredible royalties that are pouring from these sales; on the other hand, Mrs. Pachelbel is delighted about it!" [Chuck Daellenbach, from CANADIAN BRASS LIVE]

The comments from each of us are the same: there must be absolute stylistic agreement among us regarding the many two-bar phrases. For an exercise, you can identify and number each of the twenty subjects in the score; you will then be able to observe which instrument has which melody. There are indeed twenty, but no one instrument plays them all. Select points in the music where different voices have the same melody at different times, then rehearse them at the same time. For example, the first Trumpet can play bars 29 & 30, while the second Trumpet plays bars 31 & 32, and so forth. Whether the melody is played legato, detached, bright, or flowing, it must be presented in the same style in every voice. When each instrument then plays the melody at the appropriate moment in the piece, it will be played in a matching style. Most importantly, be clear about the tempo before the performance begins. The Tuba sets the tempo at the beginning of the piece, so try to maintain this tempo throughout. To do so, keep listening to the Tuba as you progress through this marvellous canon.

The Canadian Brass

3. CANON

Johann Pachelbel
(1653-1706)
arranged by Walter Barnes

1st Bb CORNET/TRUMPET

Copyright © 1988 Canadian Brass Publications, Inc., Toronto
International Copyright Secured.   All Rights Reserved.

Rondeau

JEAN JOSEPH MOURET
(1682-1738)

Mouret was a very popular composer in France during his lifetime, with more than 50 published works. Today, very little of his music is performed, with the exception of this RONDEAU. It was recently made popular because of its selection as the theme song for the BBC production *Masterpiece Theatre*. You will find, as we have, that it is an excellent addition to the brass repertoire.

The RONDEAU was originally a movement from "Fanfares pour des trompettes, timbales, violons, et hautbois" ("Fanfares for Trumpets, Kettledrums, Violins, and Oboes"). Rondo form is quite obvious: an "A" theme is presented in juxtaposition with other melodic themes. Specifically: A, A1, B, A1, C, D, A, A1.

The two Trumpets share the melody in the RONDEAU. The 2nd Trumpet part can be performed on a Piccolo Trumpet. (You might rent a Piccolo to try it; it will add a lot of spice to the quintet sound. The Yamaha 10 is a good model to start on). As in TRUMPET VOLUNTARY, and CANON, the RONDEAU melody is passed back and forth between you. You must strive for matched styles, tones, articulations, and note lengths. If the audience was not able to see you, they should think that only one trumpet is playing. When a Piccolo is used, there will necessarily be a tone change, but the new color adds to the overall texture of the piece. Beware of the octave doubling at letter D; you are subservient to the lower instruments, something uncommon in the quintet. When the two Trumpets are doubled at bar 61, take great care with intonation and matching styles.

The Canadian Brass

4. RONDEAU

Jean-Joseph Mouret
(1682-1738)
arranged by Walter Barnes

t Bb CORNET/TRUMPET

Copyright © 1988 Canadian Brass Publications, Inc., Toronto
International Copyright Secured.   All Rights Reserved.

Largo

and

Hallelujah Chorus

GEORGE FRIDERIC HANDEL
(1685-1759)

The grandeur and sustained power of Handel's oratorio style, the expressive simplicity of his melody, and the breadth and clarity of the harmonic structure form a wonderful artistic whole. He is unquestionably one of the 'great masters.' (Baker's Biographical Dictionary of Musicians)

We are sure you will enthusiastically agree with this statement after playing the two Handel compositions in this book. The LARGO (from the opera *Xerxes*, 1738) displays one of the most sustained, singing melodies imaginable. This melody is always supported by a simple harmonic bass. The HALLELUJAH CHORUS (from the oratorio *Messiah*, 1741) is best described by Handel himself. Upon completion of the "Chorus" he said, "I did think I did see all Heaven before me—and the great God himself!"

The LARGO deceptive in its simplicity. The opening fifteen bars must be very legato and smooth, while the rhythm must be constant and clear. At measure 15, the melody passes from the French Horn to the Trumpets. As in the CANON, tone, tonguing, and phrasing must be the same among all the players. Let the musical lines overlap momentarily as you pass this beautiful melody back and forth. The notes should be long and full valued. Be alert for good intonation when doubling at the unison in bars 39-43. Try to make the ending gentle with a gradual, sustained rallentando.

The HALLELUJAH CHORUS offers completely different challenges. There are two distinct styles of playing involved in this piece: long sustained phrases (for example, bars 35-41 and 58-69), and short, bright, and sharply tongued phrases (such as in bars 19-21). When playing the long, sustained phrases, it is important to give full time value to every note. Be sure to take frequent, large breaths so that the strength comes from the air and not brute force.

The Canadian Brass

5. LARGO

from *Xerxes*

1st B♭ CORNET/TRUMPET

George Frideric Handel
(1685-1759)
arranged by Walter Barnes

Copyright © 1988 Canadian Brass Publications, Inc., Toronto
International Copyright Secured.   All Rights Reserved.

6. HALLELUJAH CHORUS

from *Messiah*

George Frideric Han(del)
(1685-175..)
arranged by Walter Barr

1st B♭ CORNET/TRUMPET

Copyright © 1988 Canadian Brass Publications, Inc., Toronto
International Copyright Secured.   All Rights Reserved.

My Heart, Ever Faithful

and

Contrapunctus I from *The Art of the Fugue*

JOHANN SEBASTIAN BACH
(1685-1750)

We have selected two works of Bach that represent the wide range of this composer's brilliant talent. MY HEART EVER FAITHFUL is an aria for soprano and continuo from the Whitsunday (Pentecost) Cantata No. 68. The French Horn, Trombone, and Tuba provide the accompaniment for the two Trumpets, who toss their phrases back and forth to each other. This is a delightful, light aria that sings of unrestrained joy.

The Art of the Fugue was written at the end of Bach's life. The complete work is a thorough study of all the contrapuntal techniques that can be applied to fugal writing. Bach died before completing the last (fourteenth) fugue. The first fugue is a simple fugue, a single subject followed by its answer. Since this is such a monumental work, we wanted to include the first, most straight-forward fugue for you in this collection. We have recorded the complete *Art of the Fugue* on the CBS recording label. We hope that you will listen to the entire work, especially after conquering this fugue yourself.

The aria MY HEART EVER FAITHFUL is a study in contrasting performance styles. The continuo (French Horn, Trombone and Tuba) is bouncy, light and detached. On the other hand, the two Trumpets are performing the legato vocal line, and should therefore be smooth and singing. Pass your lines back and forth, taking care to 'hand off' your line to the next. Since the two Trumpets are doubled at the end of each phrase, be very careful with the tuning. When the piece changes style briefly at bars 37-40, do not become overly heavy. The original phrase concludes the piece, giving it a wonderful sense of completion.

The Canadian Brass

7. MY HEART, EVER FAITHFUL
from Cantata No. 68

J.S. Bach
(1685-1750)
arranged by Walter Barnes

st Bb CORNET/TRUMPET

Copyright © 1988 Canadian Brass Publications, Inc., Toronto
International Copyright Secured.   All Rights Reserved.

CONTRAPUNCTUS I (from *The Art of the Fugue*) is perhaps the most difficult selection in the book. The range is comfortable, the phrases are not too long for proper breathing, and the melodic shape is always clear. But there is always a danger of mis-counting the rests. Consider the fugue to be an endless string of notes passed from one instrument to the next. In this way, CONTRAPUNCUS I is a typical fugue transcribed for five brass instruments, so not all the voices are sounding at the same time. Therefore, someone is always waiting to re-enter. While discussing the techniques used in playing fugues, we realized that the same points were equally important for each performer.

'Listen for the continuation of other people's lines, and try to come in smoothly and confidently.'

'Make sure you know when you pick up someone else's line, and do so without a hitch.'

'Listen to the tape that we have made for you, and try to learn all the other parts of the music.'

'This is one piece in which you have to stay very alert. Listen for the continuation of other people's lines.'

'Take frequent deep breaths, play long full phrases, and listen to the tape with this book.'

The Canadian Brass

8. CONTRAPUNCTUS I
from *The Art of the Fugue*

J.S. Bach
(1685-1750)
arranged by Walter Barnes

st Bb CORNET/TRUMPET

Copyright © 1988 Canadian Brass Publications, Inc., Toronto
International Copyright Secured.   All Rights Reserved.

Andante from the Trumpet Concerto

FRANZ JOSEPH HAYDN
(1732-1809)

Haydn wrote 31 concertos during his prolific career, with the "Trumpet Concerto" (1796) being the only one that is still regularly performed. The ANDANTE is the gentle, melodic second movement between two very exciting and technically demanding movements.

The last year of Johann Sebastian Bach's life is generally accepted as the end of the Baroque Period. In the Classical era that followed, form, structure and symmetrical shape became all-important. This can be observed clearly in our selection by Haydn. We have changed the key and simplified the melodic line of the concerto movement for you. But, in our recording of this book, Ron has performed the solo trumpet part in its original embellished form. You might also want to listen to the complete recording of the Haydn "Trumpet Concerto" so that you can understand the relationship of the 2nd movement to the other two.

As already stated, I believe that you should hear the original solo Trumpet part, so that is what I have recorded for you. However, I suggest that you start with this simpler version, working gradually toward the original ANDANTE as Haydn wrote it.

Conceive of your solo line with long, smooth singing phrases, and with a simplicity of style that leaves any technical problems behind. Tune your low D's and E♭'s carefully, breathe only on rests (with the exception of bars 13-16, 21-24, and 37-40), observe the dynamic markings scrupulously, and, most importantly, play the solo beautifully!

The Canadian Brass

9. ANDANTE
from the Trumpet Concerto

Franz Joseph Haydn
(1732-1809)
arranged by Walter Barnes

Bb CORNET/TRUMPET

Copyright © 1988 Canadian Brass Publications, Inc., Toronto
International Copyright Secured.   All Rights Reserved.

Cor Royal

PHILIPP NICOLAI (1556-1608)
PETER CORNELIUS (1824-1874)

COR ROYAL (the Royal Horn) is an unusual composition in that it was co-written by composers living some 300 years apart. This new transcription for brass gives it yet another life. The "Chorale" by Nicolai (the Westphalian composer of the famous "Wachet auf") was written and harmonized as a four voice piece in 1599 to celebrate the Three Wise Men's historic journey to Israel to see the Christ child. The obbligato to the "Chorale" was written by Peter Cornelius 270 years later. Cornelius, a student and admirer of Richard Wagner, was well-known in his own time as a composer of beautiful melodies.

At the beginning of the piece, the Trumpets and Trombone present the chorale melody in unison. The second verse turns to the harmony of Nicolai when the tuba joins the others. The third verse is quite different; harmony in the four brass encircles the obbligato solo, with a syncopated ending in bars 25-26. The four of you are playing a supporting role throughout this piece, and must never overpower the solo French Horn. Rehearse the accompaniment alone, without the solo Horn part. Once again, you are trying to achieve unanimity of style. This piece especially presents a real challenge to the Trumpets; seldom do they play a supporting role for an entire composition.

The Canadian Brass

10. COR ROYAL

chorale by Philipp Nicolai (1556-1608)
obbligato melody by Peter Cornelius (1824-1874)
arranged by Walter Barnes

Bb CORNET/TRUMPET

Copyright © 1988 Canadian Brass Publications, Inc., Toronto
International Copyright Secured.   All Rights Reserved.

Sakura & Kimigayo

Traditional Japanese

The Canadian Brass has made many tours to the far East, even performing our music on the famous China Wall! It is in Japan, though, that we feel most at home. We have met many fine musicians there, and have had the opportunity to sample a great deal of Japanese traditional music. What seems unique to us about Japanese culture is the blending of so-called western music with local traditional music. It is not unusual to find modern music being played on traditional instruments, and conversely, traditional music being played on modern instruments. It is with the latter in mind that we have included two songs in this book which are very well known by all Japanese. KIMIGAYO is the "Prayer to the Emperor," and SAKURA is the famous folk song, "Cherry Blossoms." KIMIGAYO is to be used much as we would use the American or Canadian National Anthem, while SAKURA is excellent program material to be used in any performances that you give.

These two Japanese songs will give you wonderful opportunities to investigate what we consider to be our main, basic performance points for brass players.

1. AIR SUPPORT: This is the key element in all brass playing. When you get a chance, refer to our BOOK OF BEGINNING QUINTETS (the Green book) in which the first two pages talk of air support. For all brass playing, large breaths and frequent breaths are essential for good tone and tuning.
2. LISTENING: We have talked about listening throughout this book. We urge constant, careful listening to your fellow players for dynamics, blend, tuning, tempo, pulse, and doublings.
3. TIMING: Timing of notes and rests, especially the longer ones. Timing of entries and breaths, so that you are at one with your other ensemble players. Timing of thoughts and rehearsal needs, so that you are not at odds with your fellow players.
4. TONE: Your tone is your 'musical fingerprint'; only you possess that sound, only you can improve it, and only you can project that tone to your audience. Practice in front of a mirror where you can watch yourself breathing. Also, find an extremely reverberant room in which to practice from time to time (such as a concert hall, gymnasium, church, or even large bathroom) so that you can enjoy the really large sound you can make.
5. TUNING: In every text in this book, we have talked about tuning. You might have the greatest tone, but the moment you begin performing with another musician, let alone four others, intonation becomes most important. Good Intonation or tuning is only possible when you are using good air support and carefully listening to your colleagues.

We want you to be the best you can, and these five points will surely help.

The Canadian Brass

11. SAKURA
(Cherry Blossoms)

traditional Japanese
arranged by Walter Barnes

Copyright © 1988 Canadian Brass Publications, Inc., Toronto
International Copyright Secured.   All Rights Reserved.

KIMIGAYO
(Prayer to the Emperor)

traditional Japane
arranged by Walter Barr

1st B♭ CORNET/TRUMPET

Copyright © 1988 Canadian Brass Publications, Inc., Toronto
International Copyright Secured.   All Rights Reserved.

Farandole from L'Arlesienne Suite No. 2

and

Toreador Song from Carmen

GEORGES BIZET
(1838-1875)

French composer Bizet is particularly remembered today for two major works: *L'Arlesienne Suite* and the opera *Carmen*. We have chosen the most famous selection from each of these masterpieces for your quintet. Both works were written near the end of Bizet's life and feature the warmth and feeling of southern Europe. They are examples of "visual" music for brass quintet, and represent the Romantic period well.

FARANDOLE has two main themes: the first is your melody (in the minor key) at the beginning, and the second is the French Horn's at bar 17. The first theme should have a heavy effect. Don't allow the dotted rhythms (3:1 ratio) to slip into triplets (2:1 ratio). At bar 17 you are in a supporting role. In bars 26-33 and 42-49, you provide a 'bend.' In the orchestral version, which I hope you will hear; the violins play a 'glissando' by sliding their finger up the string. You will be able to produce this effect by quickly playing the two or three notes below the written note. If you use a Piccolo Trumpet for this piece, so much the better. Bars 57-62 must be in the form of a 'dialogue' between you and the other Trumpet. From 65 to the end, keep the rhythm steady, with no ritard.

The Canadian Brass

12. FARANDOLE
from L'Arlesienne Suite No. 2

Georges Bi
(1838-18
arranged by Walter Bar

1st B♭ CORNET/TRUMPET

Copyright © 1988 Canadian Brass Publications, Inc., Toronto
International Copyright Secured.   All Rights Reserved.

TOREADOR SONG features the Trombonist in your group; you are in a supporting role. The Trumpet part should be played short and staccato with a percussive effect, but don't let it get overpowering. Isolate and practice bar 41 which features a scale run. This run brings you, at last, into the the melody for four bars, followed by a counter-melody with the Trombone solo; be careful not to overpower the solo. Play right to the end of the piece without a ritard for added excitement.

The Canadian Brass

13. TOREADOR SONG

from *Carmen*

Georges Bi
(1838-18
arranged by Walter Bar

1st Bb CORNET/TRUMPET

Copyright © 1988 Canadian Brass Publications, Inc., Toronto
International Copyright Secured.   All Rights Reserved.

Hava Nagila

TRADITIONAL ISRAELI

HAVA NAGILA was originally a wordless Chassidic melody dating from the end of the nineteenth century. Chassidics were extremely orthodox Polish Jews. This song is most closely associated with the new state of Israel, as well as the national dance of Israel, the Hora.

Everyone in the quintet gets a share of the melody in this arrangement, and everyone plays a supporting role as well. The accompaniment must be bright and short. The scoring in bars 41 through 53 is extremely effective if everyone meticulously observes their entries. There is an excellent Tuba counter-melody with the first Trumpet beginning in bar 57; this same bar is the start of a faster tempo. If one of your Trumpet players can obtain a Piccolo Trumpet, then the excitement of the dance will be even greater in bar 65. The ending is most effective if you rehearse a slight accelerando, but you must stay together as one voice. Enjoy!

The Canadian Brass

14. HAVA NAGILA

traditional Israeli
arranged by Walter Barnes

st B♭ CORNET/TRUMPET

Copyright © 1988 Canadian Brass Publications, Inc., Toronto
International Copyright Secured.   All Rights Reserved.

Just a Closer Walk

arranged by DON GILLIS

This arrangement was written specifically for us to use at the beginning of our performances. Either listen to our recording <u>Canadian Brass LIVE</u>; or better still, watch our video of the same name.

In JUST A CLOSER WALK and in AMAZING GRACE, knowing a bit about the stylistic history can be helpful to ensure an appropriate performance. In times of slavery in the southern United States, death to the black person meant freedom. Death allowed a slave to 'cross the River Jordan in the Sweet Chariot, to meet God and Jesus.' During the long funeral procession out of town (since blacks were not allowed burial within the city limits) friends sang and played hymns. For variety, these hymns were played with improvised accompaniment. In this way jazz and dixieland were born. Consequently, in the presentation of both selections, you should feel a freedom of rhythm in your performance. This time the dotted eighth/sixteenth note combination needs to be played like a triplet (2:1 ratio). The melody must always be in the foreground and the accompaniment supportive. Slight bends are a nice effect in this music for all instruments, and can be applied to long notes to make them more conspicuous. After you have mastered JUST A CLOSER WALK, try playing it while you march—two steps to each bar. This will certainly aid the rhythm, and could even serve as an entrance piece for your own concerts. (A longer version of JUST A CLOSER WALK is published in our red CANADIAN BRASS ENSEMBLE SERIES series—available from your music dealer.)

The Canadian Brass

15. JUST A CLOSER WALK

traditional American
arranged by Don Gillis
adapted by Walter Barnes

1st Bb CORNET/TRUMPET

Copyright © 1988 Canadian Brass Publications, Inc., Toronto
International Copyright Secured.   All Rights Reserved.

Amazing Grace — Dixie Style
a la CANADIAN BRASS

Please read the notes for the preceding selection JUST A CLOSER WALK. The "dixie" style is imperative.

The history of this song is interesting. An American, John Newton, was a slave trader for twenty years, and a regular frequenter of taverns and bars. But, as life is ever-changing, he was converted to Evangelical Christianity, moved to England, and became a Minister of the Gospel in Liverpool. He wrote the words that have made this melody famous, and which brought it from the beer halls to the gospel halls, and, back home to the black funeral processions of New Orleans!

The second Trumpet has an unaccompanied solo for the first 16 bars of AMAZING GRACE—DIXIE STYLE. You enter, with the rest of the Quintet, playing a straight-forward version of the melody. At bar 33, the second Trumpet has a dixie version of the melody, again unaccompanied. The Quintet enters again at bar 48 in an up-beat mood. You join with the other Trumpet at 65, echoed by the French Horn and Trombone. All four of you must play exactly the same style, length of notes, and tonguing. Bar 71-72 should be the strongest note in the entire selection! Try to incorporate 'bends' in bar 73. Bar 81 is probably the most difficult chord to tune in this entire book — Beware!

We know that you and your quintet will enjoy this simplified version of Luther Henderson's arrangement which we have recorded on our album, BASIN STREET BLUES.

The Canadian Brass

16. AMAZING GRACE

traditional American
arranged by Luther Henderson
adapted by Walter Barnes

Bb CORNET/TRUMPET

Copyright © 1988 Canadian Brass Publications, Inc., Toronto
International Copyright Secured.   All Rights Reserved.